FOREWORD

When I was asked to write a foreword to this book I was incredibly flattered.

I have known Colin for a number of years and his knowledge of facts and figures is phenomenal.

His love for music and his talent for writing quiz books makes him the ideal man to pay homage to the genius that is David Bowie.

This book came about as a result of a challenge over a beer or two!

I do hope you enjoy the book.

Lloyd Cooper

1. What was David Bowie born as?
   - A. David Brown
   - B. David Jones
   - C. David Smith
   - D. David Wilson

2. When was he born?
   - A. 1945
   - B. 1946
   - C. 1947
   - D. 1948

3. Where was Bowie born?
   - A. Leicester
   - B. Lincoln
   - C. Liverpool
   - D. London

4. How old was David when he died?
   - A. 63
   - B. 65
   - C. 67
   - D. 69

5. Where did Bowie die?
   - A. Berlin
   - B. London
   - C. New York

David Bowie Quiz Book

101 Questions To Test Your Knowledge Of This Incredibly Successful Musician

Published by Glowworm Press
7 Nuffield Way
Abingdon OX14 1RL
By Colin Carter

David Bowie Quiz

This book contains one hundred and one informative and entertaining trivia questions with multiple choice answers. With 101 questions, some easy, some more demanding, this entertaining book will really test your knowledge of David Bowie.

You will be quizzed on a wide range of topics associated with Bowie for you to test yourself; with questions on his early days, his songs, his lyrics, his achievements, his awards, his charity work and much more, guaranteeing you a truly educational experience. The David Bowie Quiz Book will provide entertainment for people of all ages, and will certainly test your knowledge of this world famous musician. The book is packed with information and is a must-have for all true David Bowie fans, wherever you live in the world.

Disclaimer
All Rights Reserved. No part of this publication may be reproduced without the written permission of the publisher; with the exception of reviews written for a blog, website, magazine or newspaper. Product names referred to within this publication are the property of their respective trademark holders. This book is unofficial and is not authorised by the aforementioned interests. This book is licensed for your personal enjoyment only.

D. Paris

6. What was the name of Bowie's first wife?
    A. Abigail
    B. Alexandra
    C. Angela
    D. Aurora

7. What was the name of Bowie's first child?
    A. Damien
    B. Daniel
    C. Duncan
    D. Dustin

8. What was his son's second name?
    A. Howie
    B. Mowie
    C. Wowie
    D. Zowie

9. What unusual facial feature does Bowie appear to have?
    A. A blocked nostril
    B. Inability to grow facial hair
    C. Two different coloured eyes
    D. Two different shaped ears

10. Whom did Bowie name himself after?

A. James Bowie
B. Jeremy Bowie
C. John Bowie
D. Julian Bowie

OK, so here are the answers to the first ten questions. If you get seven or more right, you are doing very well so far, but the questions will get harder.

A1. Bowie was born as David Robert Jones.

A2. Bowie was born on 8th January 1947.

A3. Bowie was born in Brixton in London, England.

A4. Bowie died on January 10th 2016 aged just 69. He died surrounded by his family after a courageous battle with liver cancer.

A5. Bowie died at his home in New York City. His artistic work and his legacy of innovation and influence will live on forever.

A6. Bowie married his first wife Angela on 19th March 1970 at Bromley Register Office in London.

A7. David and Angie's son, born on 30th May 1971, was christened Duncan.

A8. David's son full name is Duncan Zowie Haywood Jones. He was known for some time as Zowie. He is now a film director.

A9. David was punched in the left eye in a fight at school in 1962. Bowie was in hospital for four months and had several operations before doctors determined that the damage could not be fully repaired, and David was left with a permanently dilated pupil, giving the false impression he had two different coloured eyes.

A10. As his stage name Davy Jones could be confused with Davy Jones of The Monkees, he re-named himself after James Bowie, the 19th century American pioneer who had become famous for his Bowie hunting knife. Incidentally James Bowie was killed at the infamous Battle of Alamo in 1836.

OK, back to the questions.

11. How many children did David father?
    A. 1
    B. 2
    C. 3
    D. 4

12. When did Bowie marry his second wife Iman?
    A. 1990
    B. 1992
    C. 1994
    D. 1996

13. What was the name of Bowie's first band?
    A. The Coconuts
    B. The Conduits
    C. The Koalas
    D. The Konrads

14. What is the official website address?
    A. bowie.com
    B. bowieonline.com
    C. davidbowie.com
    D. officialbowie.com

15. What was the name of Bowie's debut single?
    A. Annie May
    B. Billie Anne
    C. Liza Jane
    D. Mary Jo

16. What was the name of Bowie's debut single as a solo artist?
    A. The Chuckling Goblin
    B. The Grinning Dwarf
    C. The Laughing Gnome
    D. The Snickering Midget

17. What was the name of Bowie's debut album?
    A. A To Bowie
    B. Bowie
    C. David Bowie
    D. This is Bowie

18. What was the name of Bowie's first single to make the charts in the UK?
    A. Hallo Spaceboy
    B. Life on Mars
    C. Space Oddity
    D. Starman

19. What is the official twitter account?
    A. @Bowie
    B. @DavidBowie
    C. @DavidBowieOfficial
    D. @OfficialBowie

20. What did David wear on the cover of the UK version of 'The Man Who Sold The World'?
    A. A dress
    B. A nightie
    C. A saree
    D. A skirt

Here are the answers to the last set of questions.

A11. Bowie has two children; a son called Duncan and a daughter called Alexandria "Lexi" Zahra Jones who was born on 15th August 2000.

A12. Bowie married Somali-American model Iman in a private ceremony in Lausanne, Switzerland on 24th April 1992. His best man was his son, Duncan.

A13. Bowie formed The Konrads, his first band, in 1962 when he was aged just 15. The band played a loose form of rock and roll. It is worth tracking down 'I never dreamed' on YouTube to hear the first ever Bowie recording, with Bowie on vocals and playing saxophone,

A14. davidbowie.com is the official website. It provides a wealth of information including all the latest news, historical material and a complete discography.

A15. Bowie's debut single was called Liza Jane and was credited to Davie Jones with the King Bees, the band Bowie joined after leaving the

Konrads. It was released as a single on 5th June 1964 when Bowie was just 17 years old. The record was not a commercial success.

A16. The Laughing Gnome was David's debut single as a solo artist and was released on 14th April 1967. It used speeded up vocals and is a novelty single at best.

A17. David Bowie released his debut album entitled David Bowie on 1st June 1967. The record was not a commercial success.

A18. Space Oddity was Bowie's first single to chart in the UK. It was inspired by the film 2001: A Space Odyssey with the title of the song playing on the title of the film. The song was released on 11th July 1969, just five days before the launch of Apollo 11, which was the first manned moon landing. Space Oddity reached number five in the charts and received the 1970 Ivor Novello award for Originality.

A19. @DavidBowieOfficial is the official twitter account. It was set up in May 2009 and it has well over a million followers.

A20. On the cover of the UK version of The Man Who Sold The World album, Bowie reclined on a chaise longue in a blue and cream satin dress.

Here is the next set of questions.

21. Who covered the song 'The Man Who Sold The World' in 1974?
    A. Cilla Black
    B. Lulu
    C. Petula Clark
    D. Sandy Shaw

22. Who played immediately before Bowie at the Live Aid concert at Wembley Stadium in 1985?
    A. Elton John
    B. Queen
    C. The Who
    D. U2

23. What was the final song that Bowie sang at the Live Aid concert?
    A. Heroes
    B. Rebel Rebel
    C. TVC15
    D. Young Americans

24. Who played piano on 'Life on Mars'?
    A. Jon Anderson
    B. Bill Bruford
    C. Tony Kaye

D. Rick Wakeman

25. What was Bowie's first number one single in the UK?
    A. Fame
    B. Rebel Rebel
    C. Sound and Vision
    D. Space Oddity

26. Who was the drummer in The Spiders From Mars?
    A. Keith Moon
    B. Don Powell
    C. Roger Taylor
    D. Mick Woodmansey

27. When was Bowie indicted into the Rock and Roll Hall of Fame?
    A. 1992
    B. 1994
    C. 1996
    D. 1998

28. What song did Bowie give to Mott The Hoople?
    A. Aladdin Sane
    B. All The Young Dudes
    C. Oh! You Pretty Things

D. Suffragette City

29. What famous album did Bowie produce in 1972?
   A. Transformation
   B. Transformative
   C. Transformer
   D. Transforming

30. What was the follow up album to Ziggy Stardust?
   A. Aladdin Sane
   B. Diamond Dogs
   C. Pin Ups
   D. Station to Station

Here are the answers to the last set of questions.

A21. In January 1974, Scottish singer Lulu released a cover version of The Man Who Sold The World. She sang it in a sleazy Berlin cabaret style and the song reached number 3 in the UK charts.

A22. Bowie had the unenviable task of following Queen at the incredible Live Aid concert on 13th July 1985, but when he walked onto the stage at Wembley Stadium in his *Young Americans* suit, it was clear he was ready to put on a magnificent performance.

A23. At Live Aid, Bowie entered the stage at 8:50pm. He started with 'TVC 15' and he also performed 'Rebel Rebel', 'Modern Love' and finished his set with an amazing rendition of 'Heroes.' The concert was watched by nearly two billion people worldwide. The impresario Thomas Dolby played keyboards during the set.

A24. Legendary keyboard player Rick Wakeman played the piano on 'Life on Mars'.

He was just 21 years old at the time and was a regular session musician.

A25. The first number one single that Bowie had in the UK wasn't until 1975, when the re-release of 'Space Oddity' topped the charts. It stayed at number one for a total of five weeks.

A26. Yorkshire born Mick "Woody" Woodmansey was the drummer in the Spiders From Mars ensemble.

A27. Bowie was indicted into the Rock and Roll Hall of Fame on 17th January 1996 in a ceremony at New York's Waldorf-Astoria Hotel.

A28. 'All The Young Dudes' as recorded by Mott The Hoople is an anthem of the glam rock genre and was a huge hit. Bowie wrote the song and gave it to Mott The Hoople after he heard they were about to split due to lack of commercial success.

A29. Bowie produced 'Transformer' by Lou Reed in 1972. The album included Walk on The Wild Side, Satellite of Love and Perfect Day. The album's commercial success elevated Lou

Reed from cult status to international recognition.

A30. Released in April 1973, Aladdin Sane was the follow up album to Ziggy Stardust. The name of the album is a pun on 'A Lad Insane.'

Here is the next set of questions.

31. What was the most successful single from the Aladdin Sane album?
    A. Drive-In Saturday
    B. Let's Spend The Night Together
    C. The Jean Genie
    D. Time

32. Which album was made up exclusively of cover songs?
    A. Diamond Dogs
    B. Lodger
    C. Pin Ups
    D. Young Americans

33. What year was Bowie the best selling artist in the UK?
    A. 1973
    B. 1976
    C. 1979
    D. 1982

34. What was the most successful single from the Diamond Dogs album?
    A. Big Brother
    B. Diamond Dogs
    C. Rebel Rebel

D. Sweet Thing

35. What was the name of the TV documentary that followed Bowie on his Diamond Dogs tour?
    A. Cracked Actor
    B. Finding Fame
    C. Five Years
    D. Sound and Vision

36. What was Bowie's first number one single in the US?
    A. Fame
    B. Life on Mars
    C. Sound and Vision
    D. Space Oddity

37. How did Bowie describe the Young Americans album?
    A. British Soul
    B. Plastic Soul
    C. Rubber Soul
    D. White Soul

38. What did Bowie turn down in 2003?
    A. A knighthood
    B. Appearing on a reality TV show
    C. Reforming the Ziggy Stardust band

D. Residency at a Las Vegas hotel

39. Who worked alongside Bowie as producer on all three of the 'Berlin' albums?
    A. Brian Eno
    B. Mick Ronson
    C. Ken Scott
    D. Tony Visconti

40. Which Beatle co-wrote 'Fame'?
    A. George Harrison
    B. John Lennon
    C. Paul McCartney
    D. Ringo Starr

Here are the answers to the last block of questions.

A31. The Jean Genie was the lead single from the Aladdin Sane album and has become an iconic song with a memorable guitar riff.

A32. Released in October 1973, Pin Ups is a covers album featuring covers of songs by artists including Pink Floyd, The Kinks, The Who and The Yardbirds. The only single released from the album Sorrow was a cover of a song that was originally recorded by a band called The McCoys.

A33. 1973 was a very successful year for Bowie. He was the best selling act in the UK and at one stage he had six albums concurrently on the UK chart.

A34. Rebel Rebel was the lead single from the 1974 Diamond Dogs album. Written and produced by Bowie, it has a distinctive guitar riff that he played that once heard is never forgotten.

A35. Cracked Actor was the name of a 1975 TV documentary made by Alan Yentob featuring concert footage from the Diamond Dogs tour, whilst showing Bowie's declining mental state due to his cocaine addiction at the time.

A36. The first number one single that Bowie had in the US wasn't until 1975, when "Fame" topped the charts. and was at number one for just 2 weeks.

A37. Bowie referred to the Young Americans album as 'the definitive plastic soul record.' Bowie was widely respected by the black community in America and became one of just a few white musicians invited to perform on the TV programme Soul Train.

A38. Bowie turned down the offer of a knighthood in 2003.

A39. Tony Visconti worked alongside Bowie as producer on the Berlin trilogy of albums, Low, Heroes and Lodger.

A40. John Lennon co-wrote Fame with Bowie in 1975. It is a song that supposedly shows their dissatisfaction with fame and stardom.

I hope you're getting most of the answers right.

41. What year did Bowie headline at Glastonbury?
   A. 1980
   B. 1990
   C. 2000
   D. 2010

42. What was the name of the persona Bowie adopted during 1975 and 1976?
   A. The Thin White Dancer
   B. The Thin White Diamond
   C. The Thin White Dictator
   D. The Thin White Duke

43. What was the most successful song from the album Station to Station?
   A. Golden Years
   B. Station to Station
   C. TVC15
   D. Wild is the Wind

44. Who played in more Bowie concerts than anyone else?
   A. Carlos Alomar
   B. Gail Ann Dorsey
   C. Mike Garson

D. Mick Ronson

45. Where did Bowie live from 1976 to 1978?
    A. Austria
    B. Germany
    C. Hungary
    D. Switzerland

46. Which song includes the line 'blue blue, electric blue, that's the colour of my room.'?
    A. Beauty and the Beast
    B. Drive-In Saturday
    C. Sound and Vision
    D. Rock and Roll Suicide

47. Who sung backing vocals on Sound and Vision?
    A. Kate Bush
    B. Mary Hopkin
    C. Lulu
    D. Dusty Springfield

48. Which album's cover features Bowie in side profile wearing a duffel coat, against an orange background?
    A. Heathen
    B. Hunky Dory
    C. Lodger

D. Low

49. Which album featured the song Ashes to Ashes?
- A. Earthling
- B. Scary Monsters (and Super Creeps)
- C. Space Oddity
- D. The Man Who Sold The World

50. Who played lead guitar on Heroes?
- A. Carlos Alomar
- B. Brian Eno
- C. Robert Fripp
- D. George Murray

Here are the answers to the last set of questions.

A41. Bowie's headline performance at Glastonbury in 2000 is widely regarded as one of the best sets in the music festival's long history. A reported quarter of a million people packed into the Pyramid stage field to watch what festival founder Michael Eavis has said was his favourite ever Glastonbury set.

A42. The Thin White Duke was the persona Bowie adopted in 1975 and 1976. At that time, he was very thin due to his diet and excessive use of cocaine. His stage performances at the time were unflamboyant and he normally wore a white shirt, grey waistcoat and black trousers.

A43. Golden Years was released in November 1975 as the lead single to the Station to Station album which was released in 1976. Golden Years was the most successful of the five singles from the album.

A44. Mike Garson was Bowie's most frequent band member. He played in over 1,000 concerts around the world including Bowie's first and last concerts in the US. He played on more than twenty Bowie albums and is fondly remembered for the avant-garde piano solo on Aladdin Sane.

A45. Bowie lived in Berlin, from 1976 to 1978. He cited his interest in the German music scene as well as a need to escape his drug addiction as the reason for his move away from Los Angeles. Whilst in Berlin, he shared an apartment with Iggy Pop.

A46. The lyric 'Blue, blue, electric blue, that's the colour of my room where I will live' comes from Sound and Vision.

A47. Mary Hopkin sang backing vocals on Sound and Vision. At the time the song was recorded, she was the producer Tony Visconti's wife.

A48. Low features a side profile of Bowie wearing a duffle coat. The image was meant to be a visual pun on 'low profile'.

A49. Ashes to Ashes was on the Scary Monsters (and Super Creeps) album.

A50. Robert Fripp played lead guitar on Heroes. Carlo Alomar played rhythm guitar and George Murray played bass guitar.

I hope you're learning some new facts about Bowie, and here is the next set of questions.

51. Which song did Mick Jagger duet with Bowie?
    A. Dancing Queen
    B. Dancing in the Street
    C. John I'm Only Dancing
    D. You Should Be Dancing

52. What did Bowie sing with Queen?
    A. No Pressure
    B. Peer Pressure
    C. Pressure Cooker
    D. Under Pressure

53. How many Grammy awards has Bowie won?
    A. 3
    B. 4
    C. 5
    D. 6

54. Which of these is a popular David Bowie tribute act?
    A. Always Bowie
    B. Endless Bowie
    C. Forever Bowie

D. Ultimate Bowie

55. Which song includes the line 'It's a crash course for the ravers'?
   A. Beauty and the Beast
   B. Drive-In Saturday
   C. Rebel Rebel
   D. Rock and Roll Suicide

56. How many singles did Bowie release in his career?
   A. 95
   B. 105
   C. 115
   D. 125

57. What was the name of Bowie's last album?
   A. Blackstar
   B. Heathen
   C. Reality
   D. The Next Day

58. What was the most successful single from the album Lodger?
   A. Boys Keep Swinging
   B. DJ
   C. Look Back in Anger
   D. Yassassin

59. What song was used as an unofficial anthem for team GB during the 2012 Olympic Games?
- A. Fame
- B. Golden Years
- C. Heroes
- D. Let's Dance

60. What was the Broadway play Bowie took the title role of in 1980?
- A. Major Tom
- B. The Elephant Man
- C. The Man Who Fell To Earth
- D. The Music Man

Here are the answers to the last set of questions.

A51. Dancing in the Street was recorded by Bowie and Mick Jagger in 1985 to raise money for the Live Aid famine relief cause. The song topped the UK chart for four weeks.

A52. Under Pressure was recorded by Queen and Bowie and was released in 1981 to critical acclaim, and went on to achieve commercial success.

A53. Bowie has won a total of six Grammy awards, including a Lifetime Achievement Award in 2006.

A54. There are a number of Bowie tribute acts, but perhaps the best known is Ultimate Bowie. While there can only be one Bowie of course, Paul Bacon who brands himself as Ultimate Bowie does a convincing job of looking and sounding like Bowie. His Ultimate Bowie tribute act is so popular, he typically plays over 100 gigs a year.

A55. The lyric 'It's a crash course for the ravers' comes from Drive-In Saturday.

A56. The commonly accepted number of singles that Bowie released during his career is 125.

A57. Blackstar was Bowie's last album, released on 8th January 2016, just days before his death. It went on to become a huge commercial success reaching number one in many countries including Australia, Germany, the UK and the US.

A58. Boys Keep Swinging was the most successful single from the album Lodger. During the recording, the musicians swapped instruments – so drummer Dennis Davis played guitar whilst guitarist Carlos Alomar played drums.

A59. Heroes was used as an unofficial anthem for Team GB during the 2012 Olympic Games. The song also accompanied the parade of the British athletes at the very moving opening ceremony.

A60. In 1980 Bowie triumphed with his stunning performance as The Elephant Man at The Booth Theatre in New York City. He received unanimous praise for his acting in what was the hottest show on Broadway at the time.

Let's give you some easier questions.

61. What did Bowie say he lived on during the mid 1970s?
    A. Cocaine, milk and peppers
    B. Marijuana, yogurt and chillies
    C. Heroin, cream and tomatoes
    D. Uppers, kimchi and olives

62. Which song starts with the lyrics 'Still don't know what I was looking for'?
    A. Changes
    B. Loving The Alien
    C. Rebel Rebel
    D. Wild is the Wind

63. Who co-produced the album Let's Dance?
    A. Gus Dudgeon
    B. Nile Rogers
    C. Ken Scott
    D. Tony Visconti

64. Who played lead guitar on the album Let's Dance?
    A. Jeff Beck
    B. Nile Rodgers
    C. Carmine Rojas
    D. Stevie Ray Vaughan

65. Where was the music video to Let's Dance filmed?
- A. Australia
- B. Canada
- C. New Zealand
- D. South Africa

66. How tall was Bowie?
- A. 5 feet 6 inches
- B. 5 feet 8 inches
- C. 5 feet 10 inches
- D. 6 feet

67. Which music video features Bowie in a Pierrot clown costume?
- A. Ashes to Ashes
- B. Fashion
- C. This is not America
- D. Wild is the Wind

68. Who did Bowie duet with on 'Peace on Earth/Little Drummer Boy'?
- A. Perry Como
- B. Bing Crosby
- C. Dean Martin
- D. Andy Williams

69. What was the name of the tour in support of 'Let's Dance'?
- A. The Serious Gaslight Tour
- B. The Serious Moonlight Tour
- C. The Serious Sunlight Tour
- D. The Serious Twilight Tour

70. What was the name of the band Bowie formed in 1989?
- A. Bronze Engine
- B. Copper Contraption
- C. Tin Machine
- D. Zinc Motor

Here are the answers to the last ten questions.

A61. Bowie declared that whilst living in Los Angeles in 1975 he lived on a diet of cocaine, milk and red peppers.

A62. Changes starts with 'Still don't know what I was waiting for, and my time was running wild, a million dead end streets and every time I thought I'd got it made it seemed the taste was not so sweet.' The lyrics to the song are often seen to reflect Bowie's chameleon like personality. Musically the song features a distinctive piano riff played by Rick Wakeman.

A63. Niles Rodgers co-produced the magnificent Let's Dance album.

A64. Stevie Ray Vaughan played lead guitar on the Let's Dance album.

A65. The music video to Let's Dance was made on location in Australia. Part of the filming occurs in a bar in a 'town' with a population of less than 200 people in a remote part of New South Wales.

A66. David Bowie was 5 feet 10 inches tall.

A67. Bowie wore a Pierrot costume in the video for Ashes to Ashes. At the time when it was made in 1980, it was the most expensive music video ever made, and it was the first video that cost more than half a million dollars to make.

A68. The unlikely pairing of Bowie and Bing Crosby came together for a recording in 1977 for a Bing Crosby Christmas Special TV show. The resulting single Peace on Earth/Little Drummer Boy was released in 1982 and went on to be very successful, selling over 400,000 copies in the UK alone. The song is now regarded as a Christmas classic in many countries.

A69. The name of the 1983 global tour in support of the album 'Let's Dance' was of course The Serious Moonlight Tour.

A70. Bowie formed rock band Tin Machine as a quartet in 1989. The band recorded two studio albums and one live album before dissolving in 1992 having sold over two million albums.

Here is a set of questions on films that David has appeared in.

71. What was the first feature film Bowie appeared in?
    A. Christiane F.
    B. The Hunger
    C. The Man Who Fell To Earth
    D. Virgin Soldiers

72. What was the name of the 1986 movie Bowie starred in featuring Patsy Kensit and Sade?
    A. Absolute Bananas
    B. Absolute Beginners
    C. Absolute Nonsense
    D. Absolutely Fabulous

73. Where was the movie Just a Gigolo set?
    A. Berlin
    B. Frankfurt
    C. Hamburg
    D. Munich

74. What role die Bowie play in The Last Temptation of Christ?
    A. John the Baptist
    B. Judas Iscariot

C. Pontius Pilate
D. Zebedee

75. Who did Bowie portray in the 1996 film Basquiat?
    A. Keith Haring
    B. David Hockney
    C. Roy Lichtenstein
    D. Andy Warhol

76. Who was Bowie's co-star in The Hunger?
    A. Brigitte Bardot
    B. Juliette Binoche
    C. Carole Bouquet
    D. Catherine Deneuve

77. What part did Bowie play in the 2006 science-fiction thriller The Prestige?
    A. Tim Berners-Lee
    B. Thomas Edison
    C. Alexander Fleming
    D. Nikola Tesla

78. When was Merry Christmas, Mr. Lawrence released?
    A. 1981
    B. 1983
    C. 1985

D. 1987

79. What was the name of the movie where Bowie played the part of Jareth The Goblin King?
- A. The Dark Crystal
- B. Dungeons and Dragons
- C. Hellboy
- D. Labyrinth

80. What was the name of the 1976 science fiction film starring Bowie?
- A. The Man from UNCLE
- B. The Man Who Fell To Earth
- C. The Man Who Knew Too Much
- D. The Man Who Would Be King

Here are the answers to the set of movie related questions.

A71. The first feature film Bowie appeared in was the 1969 British war-comedy film Virgin Soldiers. The film was based on a novel of the same name by Leslie Thomas and the cast included Hywel Bennett, Nigel Davenport and Lynn Redgrave.

A72. Absolute Beginners was the title of a 1986 musical starring Bowie, Ray Davies, James Fox, Patsy Kensit, Sade and others. It was a box office failure but the theme song was popular reaching number 2 in the UK charts.

A73. Just a Gigolo was set in Berlin. As well as Bowie, it starred Marlene Dietrich, Kim Novak and Sydne Rome.

A74. The 1988 movie The Last Temptation of Christ, directed by Martin Scorsese, cast Bowie as Pontius Pilate.

A75. Bowie played the role of Andy Warhol in Basquiat. As well as Bowie the film featured Willem Dafoe, Dennis Hopper, Courtney Love,

Gary Oldman, Tatum O'Neal and Christopher Walken.

A76. Catherine Deneuve played alongside Bowie in the 1983 erotic horror film The Hunger. Also playing an important role was Susan Sarandon.

A77. Bowie played the role of Nikola Tesla in the 2006 movie The Prestige. The movie also starred Christian Bale, Michael Caine, Hugh Jackman and Scarlett Johansson.

A78. Merry Christmas, Mr. Lawrence was released in 1983. It is set in a Japanese prisoner of war camp and is particularly noted for its soundtrack The film is one of very few P.O.W films where an escape does not feature as a prominent storyline.

A79. Labyrinth was an elaborate musical fantasy film with Bowie starring as the Goblin King. The movie was directed by Jim Henson with George Lucas as executive producer and its screenplay was by Terry Jones.

A80. The Man Who Fell To Earth is the name of the cult 1976 science fiction film directed by

Nicola Roeg featuring Bowie as a humanoid alien who has come to Earth on a mission to take water back to his planet which is suffering from a devastating drought.

Here are the next set of questions, let's hope you get most of them right.

81. What was the opening track on the Let's Dance album?
    A. Criminal World
    B. Modern Love
    C. Ricochet
    D. Without You

82. Who originally recorded China Girl?
    A. Nick Cave
    B. Elvis Costello
    C. Gary Numan
    D. Iggy Pop

83. What was nominated for the Best Original Motion Picture Song at the 1982 Golden Globe Awards?
    A. Absolute Beginners
    B. Cat People
    C. Life On Mars
    D. Modern Love

84. What was the name of the concert film filmed in Australia and released in 1987?
    A. Angry Spider
    B. Glass Spider

    C. Hairy Spider
    D. Poisonous Spider

85. Which famous guitarist went to the same school as Bowie?
    A. Eric Clapton
    B. Peter Frampton
    C. Brian May
    D. Pete Townshend

86. What society did Bowie become the founder of, aged just 17?
    A. Prevention of cruelty to aliens
    B. Prevention of cruelty to bearded men
    C. Prevention of cruelty to gnomes
    D. Prevention of cruelty to long haired men

87. Which song contains the line 'If you say run, I'll run with you, and if you say hide, I'll hide with you'?
    A. Dead Man Walking
    B. Let's Dance
    C. Never Let Me Down
    D. Underground

88. What was the first musical instrument Bowie learnt to play?
    A. Cello
    B. Guitar
    C. Piano
    D. Saxophone

89. What song did Bowie sing in Ricky Gervais's TV programme Extras in 2006?
    A. Bloated National Joke
    B. Chubby Little Loser
    C. Depressed and Useless
    D. Sold Out Dreamer

90. Which member of the Rolling Stones is name-checked in 'Drive-In Saturday'?
    A. Mick Jagger
    B. Keith Richards
    C. Charlie Watts
    D. Ronnie Wood

Here are the answers to the last set of questions.

A81. Modern Love was the first track on the Let's Dance album. It is a very powerful opening track, and its single release was a commercial success too.

A82. China Girl was co-written by Iggy Pop and Bowie during their time in Berlin, and appeared on Pop's solo album 'The Idiot' in 1977. Niles Rodgers produced a polished re-recorded version of the song for Bowie in 1982 which became a major hit.

A83. The theme song Cat People (Putting Out Fire) was nominated for the Best Original Motion Picture Song at the 1982 Golden Globe Awards for the movie Cat People starring the stunning Nastassja Kinski. The song was later used in Quentin Tarantino's 2009 film Inglourious Basterds.

A84. Glass Spider is the name of the concert film filmed over the course of eight shows in Australia in November 1987 during the Glass Spider Tour. It has been widely reported that it influenced many other artists including Britney Spears, Madonna and U2 on their own tours.

A85. Peter Frampton attended Bromley Technical High School at the same time as Bowie and they often jammed together. They went on to develop a life long friendship.

A86. In 1964, aged just 17, David appeared on the BBC show Tonight, fronted by Cliff Michelmore, to announce he had formed 'The society for prevention of cruelty to long haired men'. During the show Bowie said, "I think we're all fairly tolerant but for the last two years, we've had comments like 'Darling!' and 'Can I carry your handbag?' thrown at us, and I think it just has to stop now."

A87. The line 'If you say run, I'll run with you, and if you say hide, I'll hide with you.' is from Let's Dance, written and recorded in 1972.

A88. The first musical instrument Bowie learned to play was a saxophone; he started playing sax when he was just twelve years old.

A89. David demonstrated his comedic talents by composing a ditty called 'Chubby Little

Loser' in the Extras episode he features in. The song is also known as Pug Nose Face and Little Fat Man. It is worth tracking the clip down on YouTube.

A90. Mick Jagger is name-checked on the song 'Drive-In Saturday'. The lyrics included "When people stared in Jagger's eyes and scored".

Here is the final set of questions. Enjoy!

91. Which song does Major Tom *not* appear in?
    A. Ashes to Ashes
    B. Hallo Spaceboy
    C. Space Oddity
    D. Starman

92. Which of these songs appears on the album 'Hours'?
    A. Three
    B. Five
    C. Seven
    D. Nine

93. What does Bowie wear on the cover of the album 'Earthling'?
    A. A 1950s style leather jacket
    B. A mink fur coat
    C. A plastic raincoat
    D. A Union Jack coat

94. How many of Bowie's albums does not have an image of him on the cover?
    A. 0
    B. 2
    C. 4

D. 6

95. What does Bowie's wife Iman have tattooed on her leg?
    A. A Bowie Knife
    B. Heroes
    C. Modern Love
    D. Starman

96. What album featured the single Blue Jean?
    A. Love You Till Tuesday
    B. Outside
    C. Reality
    D. Tonight

97. What is Bowie's most successful album of all time?
    A. Blackstar
    B. changesbowie
    C. Let's Dance
    D. The Rise and Fall of Ziggy Stardust and the Spiders From Mars

98. Which song contains the line 'He's outrageous, he screams and he bawls'?
    A. Boys Keep Swinging
    B. Breaking Glass

        C. Healing Hands
        D. The Jean Genie

99. What was the last single released during Bowie's lifetime?
        A. I Can't Give Everything Away
        B. Lazarus
        C. Valentine's Day
        D. Where Are We Now?

100. When was Bowie's final live performance?
        A. 2006
        B. 2008
        C. 2010
        D. 2012

101. What was the last song Bowie sang live?
        A. Ashes To Ashes
        B. Changes
        C. Golden Years
        D. Rebel Rebel

Here are the answers to the last set of questions.

A91. The fictional character of Major Tom appeared in three Bowie songs – Space Oddity, Ashes to Ashes and Hallo Spaceboy.

A92. Seven is a song that appears on the album 'Hours' in 1999. It was released as a single in 2000. As an aside, the song was originally written for the computer game Omikron.

A93. One of Bowie's many iconic looks was a Union Jack outsized coat made for him by British designer Alexander McQueen, made in 1996 when McQueen was still relatively unknown. He originally created the coat as a tour costume but Bowie was so impressed by it, he decided to wear it on the cover of his next album, Earthling.

A94. Bowie released 27 studio albums and 21 live albums. An image of Bowie appears on all of his album covers except two – 'Blackstar' and some versions of the UK release of 'The Buddha of Suburbia.' Give yourself a bonus point if you knew that. It is interesting to look through his album covers and see how his image constantly changed over the years.

A95. Iman has an image of a Bowie knife tattooed on her ankle, with 'David' written on the handle.

A96. Blue Jean was the first single taken from the album 'Tonight' released in 1984. The song is loosely inspired by Eddie Cochrane. An accompanying short film for the song entitled 'Jazzin' for Blue Jean' won the 1985 Grammy Award for "Best Video, Short Form" and is worth tracking down on YouTube.

A97. Let's Dance was Bowie's best selling album with well over 10 million copies sold worldwide.

A98. The lyric 'He's outrageous, he screams and he bawls' are from "The Jean Genie". Its title is an illusion to French author Jean Genet. The song was recorded in New York City in 1972 and became one of Bowie's best loved songs.

A99. Lazarus was the last single to be released during Bowie's lifetime. It was the second single from the Blackstar album and was released on 17th December 2015.

A100. His final live performance was at the Black Ball, a charity event for Keep a Child Alive held at the Hammerstein Ballroom in Manhattan, New York on 9th November 2006.

A101. 'Changes' was the last song Bowie performed live on stage.

That's it. I hope you enjoyed this book, and I hope you got most of the answers right. I also hope you learnt a few new things about the incredible man and musician that was David Bowie.

If you saw anything wrong, or if you have any comments, please get in touch via the glowwormpress.com website.

Thanks for reading, and if you did enjoy the book, please leave a positive review on Amazon.

Printed in Great Britain
by Amazon